AT LAST, A BOOK THAT
YOU CAN GIVE TO YOUR CAT!

If you suspect that yoga is something that your cat can derive great pleasure from, then you will find your intuition confirmed by this original, thoroughly witty, illustrated yoga book for cats. Finally, the modern house cat need not deny him- or herself the fruits of yoga meditation and Oriental wisdom. Now your friendly kitty can reach a higher, more satisfying state of being—through yoga practice. This exuberant, fun-filled feline guide will enable not only your kitty, but YOU, TOO, to reach an unforgettable cat nirvana.

YOGA
FOR
CATS

With Illustrations by

Traudl & Walter Reiner

Translated by Robert Weil

ST. MARTIN'S PAPERBACKS

*FOR FRISKY,
BOOTS,
JACKIE, AND
JED*

Published by arrangement with Wilhelm Heyne Verlag

YOGA FOR CATS

ISBN: 0-312-92438-0

Printed in the United States of America

Wilhelm Heyne edition published 1989
St. Martin's Paperbacks edition/December 1990

10 9 8 7 6 5 4 3 2 1

"The regular practice of asanas, pranayama and meditation will lead you to become a sleek, fulfilled and wise cat."

— Swami Pussananda

Felix

May Ling

Scrappy

Chester

Whiskers

Blackie

*We thank the Board of
the Yoga-Cat Institute
for its friendly support.*

Warm-Ups and Pre-Exercises

First, relax the paws and legs. Then follow
with the belly and chest, the neck, the face,
and finally with the whiskers.

Relaxation and Concentration

Shoulder Exercises

Leg and Paw Exercises

Eye Movement Number One

Sit in a relaxed position. Keep your head still while following a moving object back and forth. Only your eyes should move.

Eye Movement Number Two

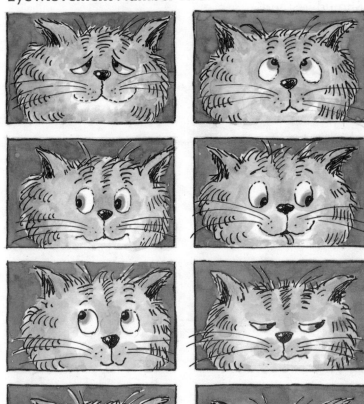

Sarvangasana
(Shoulder Stand)

Variation
(Bridge Pose)

Sirshasana
(Head Stand)

coming into the pose

full headstand

with legs outstretched

Lotus variation

Viparita Karani
(Upside-down Pose)

Hanumanasana

(Splits, or
Hanuman Pose)

Halasana
(Plow Pose)

Steps

Bhujangasana
(Cobra Pose)

Variations

Salabhasana
(Locust Pose)

Half Locust

Full Locust

Dhanurasana
(Bow Pose)

Ardha Matsyen-drasana

(Half-spinal twist)

(Named after the renowned Yoga-master Matsyendrasana)

bent leg variation

bent leg variation with
paws clasped behind back

full spinal twist

Mayurasana
(Peacock Pose)

Steps

Supta Vajrasana
(Lying-Down Diamond Pose or
Bent Pelvic Pose)

Steps

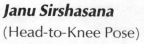

Janu Sirshasana
(Head-to-Knee Pose)

Steps

Variations

Chakrasana
(Wheel Pose)

Steps

Kurmasana
(Turtle Pose)

Steps

Chatuskonasana
(Four-Cornered Pose)

Variation

Akarna Dhanurasana
(Shooting Bow Pose)

Step

Warm-Up

Samkatasana
(Heroic Pose)

Steps

Mandukasana
(Frog Pose)

Dynamic Variation

Kutilangasana
(Snake Pose)

Setuasana
(Full Bridge Pose)

Uttan Pristhasana
(Dog Pose)

Simhasana
(Lion Pose)

Variations

Ardha Chandrasana
(Half-Moon Pose)

Garudasana
(Eagle Pose)

Variations

Vrikshasana
(Tree Pose)

Variation

Warm-Up

Natarajasana
(King Dancer's Pose)

Steps

Variations

Trikonasana
(Triangle Pose)

Steps

Dynamic Variations

Utkatasana
(Chair Pose)

Bhadrasana
(Gentle Pose)

Savasana
(Play Dead Pose)

Moves

Meditative Poses

(Full Lotus Pose)

Vajrasana
(Diamond Pose)

Virasana
(Warrior Pose)

Sukhasana
(Relaxed Pose)

Padmasana
(Lotus Position)

Warm-Ups

1. Variation

2. Variation

Padmasana
(Lotus Position)

3. Variation

Yoga Mudra
(Tied and Bound Pose)

Moves

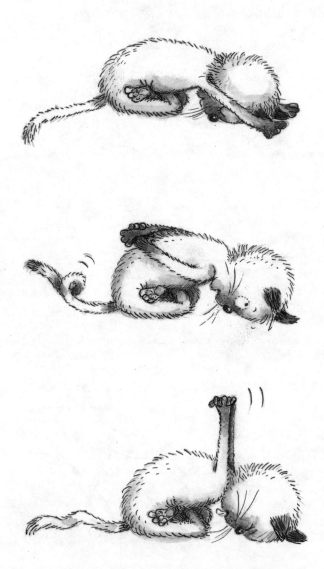

Suryanamaskar
(Sun Salute)

1 →

1 →

1 →

Uddiyana Bandha
(Stomach Hold)

Steps

Maha Bandha

(Great Lock or
Chin Lock)

Steps

Maha Veda
(Rooster Pose)

Variation

Breathe Deeply

Warm-Ups

Rhythmic Breathing

Press the diaphragm forward and let the belly expand.

Exhale, draw in the diaphragm and let the belly contract.

Pranayama
(Breathing Practices)

Alternate nostril breathing.

Eternal Wisdom for Today's Lifestyles

LINDA GOODMAN'S STAR SIGNS

Linda Goodman is the most respected name in astrology and metaphysics. With her usual compassion, wit, and perception, she has now written the definitive guide to putting established knowledge to work for all her readers in today's fast-paced world. It will lead you to discover your latent powers, to control your personal destiny, and to recall the forgotten harmony of the Universe.

LINDA GOODMAN'S STAR SIGNS
_____ 91263-3 $4.95 U.S.   _____ 91264-1 $5.95 Can.

READ
MY
LIPS.

The Wit & Wisdom of
GEORGE
BUSH

With some reflections by Dan Quayle

edited by Ken Brady & Jeremy Solomon